IMMERSION LEARNING: A TRAVELOGUE

Immersion Learning: A Travelogue

A Study of the Value of the Block Method of Teaching in Waldorf Education

FRANS LUTTERS

*Because I had the privilege of having a wonderful experience together
with others . . . I have decided to make an attempt at
a brief description of that fabulous trip . . .*
Hermann Hesse, *Journey to the East*

*The way goes on, endlessly, from the door where it began . . .
to far beyond the horizon . . .*
J. R. R. Tolkien, *The Lord of the Rings*

There can be no doubt that all our knowledge begins with experience.
Immanuel Kant, *Critique of Pure Reason*

Published by:
Waldorf Publications
351 Fairview Avenue, Unit 625
Hudson, NY 12534

© 2020 Waldorf Publications

ISBN: 978-1-943582-43-3

Translated from the Dutch by Philip Mees
Editor: Patrice Maynard
Design: J.S. Legg

Originally published in Dutch by the University for Applied Sciences
Leiden, Netherlands as *Reizen door Periodeland*, 2018.

Contents

Note: *The pronouns "he" and "him" are used to represent both genders throughout the book in keeping with the tradition of the original Dutch language.*

Introduction

Since the first Waldorf school opened her doors one hundred years ago, the morning main lesson has been a key characteristic of children's Waldorf education experience around the world. The block method of teaching for the morning main lesson is part of the teaching instruments of every Waldorf teacher. In these morning block lessons, teachers invite their pupils along on a journey. This journey typically spans several weeks. During this time, the class and teacher fully immerse in a specific topic or theme. During this immersion process pupils encounter and explore key characters, events, and questions related to the theme or topic; for instance, by listening to oral storytelling, by conducting experiments, by creating artwork or by engaging in class dialogues. All activities are deliberately chosen, well prepared, and carefully hosted by the class teacher. The primary purpose is to foster the pupils' imaginative abilities. Van Alphen (2011) examines how in Waldorf education, imagination is understood as a "transformative tool." He describes how Steiner argued that

> imagination is a heightened form of cognition, capable of transforming the knowledge and skills to be learned into enhanced experiences. These experiences stimulate creativity in thinking and involve the emotions of the learners, through which a more meaningful relationship is established with the learning material (Van Alphen, 2011, p. 16).

As such, it is understandable that the activities in the

morning main lesson are not intended to transfer factual knowledge or fixed understandings from teachers to pupils. Rather, they serve as invitations for pupils to develop a personal, heartfelt connection with the content and topic; to create a sense of wonder, of curiosity that will "tickle" pupils to become engaged in such a way that they will gradually want to give meaning to what they encounter. They serve to awaken a longing for a deep, personal understanding of the topic at hand and to gradually form flexible concepts to build this understanding. And—by engaging in this process—to gradually develop an understanding of themselves as active, intentional beings who have something of value to contribute to life in this world. Not surprisingly, Waldorf teachers and former Waldorf pupils alike, typically refer to main lessons as "quintessentially Waldorf."

In his book *The five dimensions of Waldorf education in the work of Rudolf Steiner* (2016), Valentin Wember places the morning main lessons firmly within the first dimension as one of "the Big 12" basic elements from 1919. He argues that these dimensions present the essentials of Waldorf education that will allow educators of any time and place to create the kind of education that is necessary, meaningful, and healthy for individuals as well as for the world for which they share a collective responsibility. Wember emphasizes that creating these educational experiences requires a balancing act: between preserving the convincingly tried and tested content and practices of Block method teaching while simultaneously creating a space for innovations that resonate the needs and voices of our current and future times. There is no set script to perform this balancing act and teachers of all times and places need to search for and establish their own and meaningful ways to do so.

With this book, *Immersion Learning: A Travelogue*, Frans

Lutters presents a colourful and valuable insight into how a greatly experienced teacher has taken on this challenge of creating the required balance for teaching the morning main lessons. He does so by inviting us along on a journey in which he explores the practice and workings of immersion learning through the block method of teaching. This book is the culmination of his ongoing work as a teacher and of the project Frans conducted as part of the ongoing research program "Values and Value of Waldorf Education" between 2015 and 2018. This research program was founded in 2014 as a joint initiative of the University of Applied Sciences, Leiden, the Netherlands, and Waldorf education organizations throughout Holland. It was intended to stimulate dialogue on the meaning and purposes of Waldorf education in contemporary society. The program brings together educational researchers and practitioners. Their collaborative research is intended to: build knowledge and understanding of purposes and practices in contemporary Waldorf education; explore and evaluate innovative practices in Waldorf education; and contribute to the professional development of present and future educators in Waldorf schools. Research activities are conceived and practiced as a means to develop a shared, evolving body of understanding of educational processes, teaching, and child development in the context of Waldorf education (Mayo, 2019).

When Frans started his research project, he told me he had his mind set on conducting a scientific study, based on literature review and in-depth interviews with teachers. He wanted to convey the value of the block teaching method for the morning main lessons to others, especially novice Waldorf teachers. For his work as a practitioner/researcher, Frans could put to use an impressive "toolbox" of experiences, skills, knowledge, understandings, instruments, and personal qualities he had developed through three different "roles" that ran as a red thread through his life course: that of the teacher, of the student, and of the researcher. He started the project with extensive experience and deep understanding of teaching the main lesson; years of experience as an author; and a burning passion for the topic. Not surprisingly, Frans was soon writing up his first findings from his literature review and from data collected through teacher interviews. In these writings he meticulously and objectively conveyed the observations, perspectives, and understandings of his "informants," keeping interpretation to a minimum. It came as quite a surprise, however, when a year and a half into the project, the process abruptly came to a halt. Frans indicated that he needed some time to think things over. At our following meeting Frans drew a deep breath. He told me that through his participation in the research program he had developed a new understanding of himself as an author. And, as a result, he needed to go about writing up this project in a new way. He felt that in order for this research project to be of value for novice teachers, he needed to provide them with an example of the process that *he*, as a person—a teacher, student, researcher, artist, husband, father, and many more roles combined in one—goes through as he continues to explore and develop his practices and understandings of his morning main lessons. Not in order to prescribe or explain or define for them what needs to be done, but to inspire and encourage the reader to continue to develop her or his own understandings and practices.

Frans decided to write up his research project as a "travelogue." In this travelogue Frans invites us to join him on a journey through what he refers to as "Blockland." As we set out to travel, he serves as our experienced companion. At the beginning of the journey Frans points out the lay of the land of the main lessons in contemporary Waldorf education in the Netherlands. He shares stories of his classroom routines that have taken shape over the course of nearly four decades of teaching. At first glance, the content of his lessons, the rhythm he creates through different activities, the activities themselves, are all very "classic" Waldorf, imaging one hundred years of tradition and experience. However, if you take the time to more carefully observe these images, you will discover that he has developed classroom practices that allow for what one might call "anthroposophy in action." He describes how in his lessons he strives to create an environment in which young people are invited and taught to encounter, explore, and grasp the world of the past and present as an opening to discover who they are and want to be in today's—and tomorrow's—world. Through the past, the traditions of mankind, he aims to awaken a longing in these young people to go on to discover and shape meaningful emergent futures for themselves and for the world.

Frans also invites us to come along and visit the sources that have inspired his teaching and his personal learning process as a student of life. The encounter with these sources underlines how profoundly his thinking and teaching are rooted in the anthroposophical understanding of the world and of mankind; how these sources continue to inspire and vitalize his thinking and acting in the world. The encounter also shows that he continues to further develop his understandings and concepts by engaging in an ongoing dialogue with a broad range of other perspectives and worldviews. As such, his concepts and understandings remain flexible, rather than fixed. This is further underlined as Frans presents us, his fellow travellers, with observations, reflections, and understandings elicited from his tenth and eleventh year pupils. Taking care to include *the learners' perspective* on the morning main lesson is a key aspect of Frans' process of developing his understandings and teaching practices. Not just for this book, but for his everyday classroom practices as well. By including their perspectives, Frans creates for us a similar opportunity: to develop a deeper understanding of how young learners themselves experience immersion learning. Frans' pupils provide vivid examples, not just of what they learn or develop through these experiences, but also of why this kind of learning is valuable for life in the world of today and tomorrow.

To me, one of the things that makes this journey through "Blockland" particularly interesting to anyone involved in education is that it shows that a "traditional" teaching can nonetheless offer "innovative" learning experiences for young people. Innovative, not through, for instance, the use of new technology, but rather in the sense that these experiences invite and inspire "innovation of the individual": by fostering the development of imagination, inspiration, and intuition in learners. As I worked with Frans on the research, I began to sense that this innovative quality of Frans' teaching might be related to his strong drive to engage in dialogue with people, the world, and life in general. He engages in dialogues partly because he seems to perceive them as key instruments for his development. But equally important: they bring him tremendous joy. In these dialogues Frans is willing to share his own practices and understandings with others and have them questioned and re-examined; he is sincerely interested in and open to the thoughts and practices of others; fully willing to expand and transform his and others' understandings and practices.

In this travelogue he has shared with us how he—through a research process—once more fully engaged in a meaningful dialogue about education: with himself, reflecting on his own practices and understandings; with other authors from past and present, through his review of the literature on block teaching and his understanding of his inspirational sources; with his pupils, in order to learn from their experiences and understandings; and with us, his readers, who he aims to inspire. As such, his travelogue is a testament to his lifelong journey in creating meaningful ways to make a positive contribution to the world and offers inspiration for anyone aiming to do so.

Aziza Mayo, PhD

Professor of Education, University of Applied Sciences Leiden, the Netherlands, Director of the research program "Values and Value of Waldorf Education"
Leiden, February 2020

References

Mayo, A.Y., (2019). "Research on, in and with Waldorf Education in the Netherlands." In J. Miller (Ed.) *The International Handbook for Holistic Education*. Routledge.

Van Alphen, P. (2011). "Imagination as a transformative tool in primary school education." *Research on Steiner Education*, (2), pp. 16-34.

Wember, V. (2016). *The five dimensions of Waldorf education in the work of Rudolf Steiner. Overviews, commentaries, history, perspectives.* Stratos Books.

1

Welcome to the Land of Block Teaching

T HIS IS THE REPORT OF A STUDY of the value of the block method of teaching in today's Waldorf high schools. I made the study between 2015 and 2018 under the auspices of the University for Applied Sciences, Leiden, Netherlands. And for my report I chose the special form of a travelogue.

WHY A TRAVELOGUE ABOUT BLOCK TEACHING?

In the spirit of Waldorf education I am describing my study of the immersion approach to teaching and learning in the form of a travelogue. Every new block carries children imaginatively to a new place through a new subject over several concentrated weeks. Therefore, I will refer to these places as "Blockland" from here forward, so the reader has a sense of the movement through each round of teaching through these many different "lands." As a teacher I have experienced the value of this magnificent form of education in my daily practice for many years. For me, as an experienced Waldorf school teacher, it is important to visit Blockland through immersion learning again and again.. I travel there in my role as teacher, the bringer of new stories and meaningful experiences, and also as guardian of the landscape.

And yet, every trip unfolds only in the encounter and dialog with the inhabitants of the land, the students at our schools, who are at that moment at home in that land, and know it better than anyone else. When we come together they show me which landscapes we should explore and what we need to do there. Even though they may not always be conscious of it, they are always my guides.

In my encounter with every new generation of guides I ask myself as traveler and teacher whether the familiar itineraries may perhaps need some adjustments, whether new viewpoints may have to be discovered. As I see it, during each journey our young contemporaries need to be asked, explicitly or implicitly, what their experiences and expectations are in the context of previous experiences and existing traditions. Only in this way can our mutual journey through Blockland bring us experiences that are valuable for each of us every time anew.

For me, this was not just another trip. The worldwide growth and popularity of Waldorf education demonstrates that this form of education, and its underlying premises, have kept their attraction for young parents and their children for over a hundred years. The block method forms an integral part of this, also in the view of today's students. "I think the block is a real part of the Waldorf school," wrote one of my students.

For me the block method is so valuable because through it I strongly experience that the objective of our form of education is not so much to train students for society, but rather to form them for life. It offers both students and teachers a training ground to give new form, again and again, out of joint effort, freedom and responsibility, to the way they want and are able to stand in the world. For such educational experiences a fixed mold or prescribed method does not suffice. But such experiences can indeed grow if, out of a clear intention and a deep connection with the educational themes, a teacher is willing to meet the students each day anew, and to invite them to connect with the experience in a deep way. Continued study of what this requires (expressed in real language) is therefore an inextricable part of block teaching in Waldorf schools.

The purpose of my journey was to hand to other travelers a palette of inspiring material for their orientation and evaluation of what they need in order to teach valuable blocks themselves and, at the same time, to offer an opportunity to deepen existing teaching practices. I am also hoping to make the qualities of block education visible to new generations of teachers and students, and to foster recognition of the importance of maintaining good block education.

ABOUT THE METHOD OF MY STUDY

I structured this study as an active inquiry into the practice of my own lessons, those of my colleagues in the school, and colleagues at other Waldorf schools. *"In an active study the distance between the researcher and the people being studied is small, if not non-existent."*[1] In this study I have used these teaching environments to observe very consciously what takes place in the lessons, from the perspective of the teacher as well as from that of the student. In the process I have consulted older sources, for instance, by referring to literature, but also by recalling my own prior experiences and by asking colleagues about their findings. Most of all however, I wanted to draw from new sources: the current students in our school!

In formulating the interview questions I have tried to keep them open-ended so that experiences, insights and assumptions about block teaching could be expressed in freedom. For this reason I have used two methods. The majority of students (56%) wrote freely in response to one open question: *What is the value for you of the block in the Waldorf school?* The remaining 44% filled in a form with a number of open questions about their experiences with block teaching, such as: *How did you experience block teaching in the Waldorf high school? How did block teaching address the need for knowledge, experience and activity? Looking back over your school years, how do you view the blocks relative to the subject lessons? (Can you give a concrete example?)*

The answers of the students were then analyzed according to the method of grounded theory by Aziza Mayo of the University and myself.[2] In a process of careful consideration we looked for themes and patterns in the statements of the students.

A Remarkable Itinerary Laid Out by Young Guides

In the study I asked the students to be my guides. For this reason I entered into dialog with the older students in our school about their experiences and adventures in Blockland. This led to an itinerary along eight "viewpoints," each of them showing an aspect of the value of block teaching as they experience it. I want to invite you to join me on this journey and thus come to appreciate the wonderful possibilities in the rich landscape of block teaching in high school.

During the trip the students, the current experts in the experience of block teaching, are available to us to share their insights, experiences and pointers. I have collected these by a survey with questions, oral and written, of over 150 students between the ages of 15 and 18 years about their experiences in this land, what they like about it, what they find difficult, and what they think that their time in Blockland really does for them.

The choice of students of this age was guided by the fact that they have had block teaching for a long time and can thus draw on a wealth of experience. Moreover, they are at an age when they are quite able to reflect on their personal development. They wrote frank and honest answers to the questions I asked them. From their answers I was able to identify the eight viewpoints (themes) that were repeatedly mentioned. At each viewpoint we will hear statements of students that can accompany new travelers and, hopefully, inspire them.

BEFORE WE BEGIN...

Before we start out on our itinerary along the eight viewpoints, however, I want to ask you to allow me to briefly act as your guide. I would first like to give you a sketch of the contours and the landscape of Blockland so that you can orient yourself a little. Thereafter I want to take you to the origin of this land, the springs and sources that make it so fertile. Then I will make a more detailed report of a day on one of my earlier trips so as to give you a picture of the kinds of things you can look forward to on your own journeys. I hope that this will tell you something about why every journey through this land, even if you have been there many times before, is each time again a special and awesome adventure.

I hope that when you travel through Blockland you will take this travelogue with you for inspiration. Of course I also hope that you will enjoy the landscapes that lie in front of you on the viewpoints the guides will take you to, just as I did. But most of all I am hoping that on your journey you will become inquisitive (again) and will start conversations with the inhabitants and guides you will meet yourself. That you will use these encounters on the spot, within the landscape as it unrolls itself before the eye, for your own discoveries in Blockland; and that these discoveries and encounters may help you on your way to find new itineraries and viewpoints.

A Personal Note

I owe the fact that I have kept an open heart for the inexhaustible potential and hidden qualities of Blockland for the past 35 years to Hermann Hesse's book *Journey to the East*, which I received from my father when I was sixteen and was looking desperately for a place and a school with a valuable education. In addition, J. K. Rowling, the author of the Harry Potter series, represents for me the longing of young people for an adventurous and magical education. Rowling unlocked for an entire generation the expectation that there exists a type of education which can only be found in the interval between outer facts, from "Platform Nine and Three-Quarters."

2

The Land of Block Teaching at First Sight

*"Every day begins with the block. This means that during the
first two class periods the students are intensively focused on
one subject."* [3]

*"The subject is collectively presented to the class, but offers
many possibilities to be individualized and differentiated.
The material is carefully geared to the age and developmental
phase of the students. The questions and interests of the
students and teachers form the basis of a personal relationship
to the lesson material."* [4]

The Place and Function of the Block Method of Teaching In the High School Curriculum of Waldorf Education

For over a hundred years, Waldorf school students have been starting their day with the morning block, also called block education. In an uninterrupted line from first grade to twelfth, block teaching is practiced with students from 6 to 18 years of age. Every block deals with subjects that correspond with the themes of development that are of central importance in the daily lives of the students in the different grades. The subjects presented in the blocks are always tuned to the age of the student. Block teaching makes it possible for the student to make a profound connection with the lesson material. The students work with the lesson material in their main lesson books and thus write their own text books, as it were. Block teaching with its rich themes is followed by all students. Thus each student is offered a broad framework for his development, and also an opportunity to come to know himself better.

In block teaching, students and teacher go to work on a theme during an uninterrupted, intensive lesson period. Blocks vary in length between two and six weeks, but most blocks take three weeks. This structure makes it possible to offer the students time for immersion into the content of a particular subject by means of experiences, artistic work, collaboration, interchange, and their own research.

Block teaching creates, par excellence, the potential and time to build on the central premises of Waldorf pedagogy. With this I mean to say that block teaching offers time and space to address head, heart and hands within the learning process. I am also alluding to the fact that the arrangement and sequence of subjects in block teaching are anchored in the curriculum in such a way as to offer the students a broad field of development.[5] Before I clarify these two points I have to give you a picture of the educational vision underlying Waldorf education.

EDUCATION FOCUSED ON THE DEVELOPMENT OF THINKING, FEELING AND WILLING

The education in Waldorf schools is based on an anthropology and on insights into the human being developed by Rudolf Steiner. Fundamental to the way Waldorf education is structured is a pedagogical vision that wants to address the student in his full humanity, i.e. as a complete human being in his thinking, feeling and will. A. Krijger wrote about this:

> In this picture it is the soul—with its active forces of thinking, feeling and the will—that connects the spirit (the I) and the body in their encounter with the world, and attunes them to each other. As the soul gains in strength, the I is more consciously experienced as our deepest inner reality, and thus also the individual life intention. Upbringing and education aim to make the soul strong for this task and are therefore oriented toward developing thinking, feeling and the will. For this reason, the development of these three soul forces is the central focus of Waldorf education.[6]

In the vision underlying Waldorf education lives the view that experience (feeling) and artistic processing (will) benefit the forming of concepts (thinking), and serve the social capacities and health of the students.[7] When viewed out of this vision it is not surprising that the central focus is not only on the content of the lesson material, but also, and quite particularly, on the development of these soul forces (thinking, feeling and will) by means of the encounter with this lesson material and of the way this encounter takes place.[8]

One could also say that in the vision of Waldorf education lesson material is a means while development is the goal; for this reason what in other forms of education is called lesson material is often called developmental material in Waldorf schools. In her doctoral dissertation, H. Steenbergen calls block teaching a good example of how Waldorf schools present this developmental material. She states that the intention of block teaching is to offer learning experiences in which the students intensively focus for a longer time on one subject, so that they can go into it in depth. Because both students and teacher deeply immerse themselves in the material during the block, one strives to stimulate a personal relationship with the material. The contents of the different blocks are coordinated and offer a broad framework for development and for growing self-knowledge.[9]

DOING, EXPERIENCING AND UNDERSTANDING AS FORMATIVE PROCESSES

In the course of every block, the high school curriculum works out of the contents of the lesson and collaborative activities, via experience and artistic processing, toward the student's own conceptual understanding. To this end, the teaching processes in the block lessons aim to actively offer opportunity for the autonomous formation of concepts (thinking), experiencing things (feeling), and doing things (will). The specific structure, content and work processes in block teaching expressly create time and space to address the head (thinking), the heart (feeling), and the hands (will) within the teaching process.

Usually, the blocks are given at the beginning of the school day, because that is the time when the students, refreshed by the night, begin the day. Two uninterrupted periods give the time needed to structure the lesson with meaningful variation, because it is not deemed healthy to be doing the same thing for two hours.[10] The purpose of the alternating ways of working used during the blocks is to achieve an intense experience and connection with the subject, for instance, by precisely observing and performing experiments, creating artistic images and pictures, and observing processes in nature. In addition, time is dedicated to the spoken word, such as listening to a story told by the teacher, participating in a class discussion, drama, singing, or reciting poems. And finally, there is time for working with what was experienced in a notebook called the main lesson book using written text, drawings, painting or collages. The goal of this variety of different ways of working is to awaken, develop and support an esthetic and intuitive disposition in the students.

Each block has a specific subject that is part of the developmental themes within the various classes and is appropriate in the developmental phase of the students. The idea is that the students can in this way be addressed from certain themes in the period when they are (most) receptive to them. The aim is not only to foster the intellectual development of the students, but to offer them a broad palette for their overall health.

A distinction is made in the curriculum between developmental material and practice material. The practice material is part of the basic education as this is demanded by the State, while in the developmental material the developmental aims of Waldorf education comes to expression. The purpose of developmental material is to create a cohesive and balanced development of the three realms of thinking, feeling and the will. In the practice material skills are trained for head, heart, and hands.[11]

In block teaching the central purpose is not the transfer of specific knowledge or acquisition of skills, but the students' own personal conceptual understanding. In block education development of knowledge is the result of collective experiences and activities in which the feeling life and creativity of the students are always also addressed. Although this principle holds true as well for the subject lessons later in the day, there is in these lessons less opportunity to organize the material in this manner. An important reason for this is that one has less freedom, for instance, in the choice of lesson material. In those schools controlled by government mandates, teachers especially feel considerable time pressure to deal with the mandatory lesson material needed for standardized tests. In addition, some subjects demand more practice than block lessons. For example, in languages it is necessary to develop vocabulary and acquire familiarity with grammar.

CONTENT OF A BLOCK

The content of a block and the suitable processing methods are developed by the teacher himself. In this way the teacher is addressed in his virtuosity and professional competence, and he also receives the opportunity to manifest himself there. Although blocks always have a specific subject with the concomitant proficiency which the students get to know and learn to practice, the actual course of the lessons in block teaching is relatively open. Both students and teachers are free to bring in their own content and experiences. Thus the experience of the lesson content is realized and formed in the interaction between students and teacher. This gives to block education the character of a studio, and offers the teachers, together with their students, the freedom and potential of jointly owning the learning process.

3

The Origin of the Land of Block Teaching

"Educational-pedagogical interest ultimately consists of being interested in the unique and radically new coming into the world; this means that educational philosophy must always take into account that which cannot be foreseen, the domain that transcends the possible." [12]

BLOCK EDUCATION AS PERSONALITY-FORMING EXPERIENCE

Waldorf education came into being about a hundred years ago out of an intention to create an environment in which the students, gradually and each in his or her own way, could develop the capacity and the will to stand in and with the world out of their own inner freedom, solidarity and sense of justice, and to contribute in a positive manner to existence in the world.[13] This is a grown-up form of standing in the world in which we are willing to weigh whether what we want is also desirable for our life and that of others.[14] Waldorf education therefore aims to be a personality-forming education.[15]

Educationist G. Biesta states that the objective of teaching in personality-forming education is indeed to form the personality, but always out of an intention that contributes to fostering the desire to be a grown-up person.[16] Wanting to be a person is not something you can prescribe or force onto the students; rather it can be brought to realization by each one of them in their own way, in their own time, and out of their own potential and challenges. Education that sets this as its goal is therefore par excellence "risky" education.[17] This demands teachers who are capable and willing to meet the student with a pedagogical state of mind as a unique individual who acts, thinks and feels on his own, and is able to choose to go with the flow or to resist, while weighing time and again in himself what is desirable. As individuals we are able to create good things while also bringing meaning into these things; and out of our personal development we are also able to experience "that it is good."

THE I COMES TO MANIFESTATION

The way to adulthood to which Waldorf education aims to contribute is connected with the coming to manifestation of the subject, the individual, *the I*, in the world. Rudolf Steiner, the founder, along with Emil Molt, of Waldorf education, based his pedagogical views on a specific image of the human being, which he called the threefold human being.

This threefoldness consists of *body, soul* and *spirit*. Within the human form the head, trunk and limbs are the physical basis for respectively thinking, feeling, and the will.[18] The individual human being as acting person in the world is related by Steiner to the *spiritual* nature of the I.

The words *individuality* and *I* are used interchangeably by Steiner. For him the I is the individual, creative and spiritual principle that makes each human being unique.[19] Around age three, the child says "I" to itself for the first time. The I gives form and content to the soul; it gives us our identity, and meaning to our existence in the world. It gives direction to our many observations, feelings and experiences and is our helmsman on the ocean of life. The I has a unique history that reaches back beyond the boundaries of birth and death. It is the evolutionary principle that develops into the future based on its spiritual nature. According to Steiner, the I is therefore the inexhaustible renewer, and is the prerequisite for authentic, autonomous thinking, feeling and acting.

THE EVOLUTION OF THE HUMAN INDIVIDUAL ENTITY

Rudolf Steiner was thus an advocate of the ever-progressing evolution of the human personality. He formulated as the basic idea underlying good education the value of the never-ending becoming of the individual as imperishable I. Within the home of his language, German, he concurred with a famous work of the author and philosopher Gotthold Lessing who, in his book *The Education of the Human Race*, formulated in the late 18th century the emancipated worth of the autonomously learning individual.

Lessing conquered a new continent within European thinking in relation to *being* and *eternity*. Like a new Columbus he transcended in his thinking the boundaries of birth and death, as these had been set in the European Middle

15

Ages by Church and science. He defended the logic of the continuing development of the individual out of a broad view of upbringing and education that was shocking in its time. *"Why would I not come back as often as I can acquire new knowledge and new capacities?"*[20]

After Lessing followed Gustav Widenmann in 1861 with his prize essay *Thoughts about Immortality as Multiple Earth Lives*, which posits the value and paradigm of continuing evolution of the human spirit as unique individuality.[21] The individuation of the student as the pedagogical task of meaningful education can receive a broader perspective by this unusual paradigm.

FATHOMING THE RIDDLE

Rudolf Steiner defended a broad evolutionary paradigm. It is one of the essential premises of Waldorf pedagogy. But still, this premise is not often discussed in pedagogical practice when teachers, parents and students meet. Waldorf school teachers handle this paradigm in individual ways, and it is not a daily subject of discussion along colleagues. As a conceivable paradigm, however, it does give the teachers deep respect for *the coming to manifestation of the other*, the student. Because of this, the paradigm has an essential influence on the daily practice of education in Waldorf schools in which respect for the *uniqueness of the other* is a guiding factor. In daily practice in Dutch Waldorf schools worldwide, this paradigm is sketched in a few words during a brief meeting of the teachers at the beginning of the school day: "From the world of spirit this child is descended to you; you are to fathom his/her riddle, from day to day, from hour to hour." After this brief moment of tuning into each other, the day begins with the block in the class. This gives the teacher a mood of anticipation regarding the student, as of a newly arrived person.

Plato describes in *The Republic* that young people, from birth, may trust in themselves as sources of new capacities and insights.[22] He speaks of capacities that we bring with us at birth; they well up in the soul, as it were, like water from a spring. Socrates, Plato's teacher, treated these capacities very concretely. He viewed himself as the midwife of the spiritual power in the soul. By intensively questioning his students he helped them to enter into the world in an authentic way. Already the pre-Socratic philosophers, such as Heraclitus, Pythagoras and Empedocles, connected authenticity with the conviction that the human spirit is immortal and sets itself new goals of learning and development in successive earth lives.[23]

Heraclitus of Ephesus was the outspoken representative of metempsychosis, reincarnation. He described successive lives as a river in which everything flows: *panta rhei*. Each life poses new challenges and potential, nothing repeats itself. In Heraclitus' view each life is authentic and undetermined. It should be seen as a new project, with new intentions and opportunities, without external predestination, but rather with an *internal destiny* that unfolds itself from the moment of birth. The concepts of the classical Greek thinkers point in a direction that can be helpful in the broadening and reformulation of a respectful pedagogy.

John Caputo, with his theology of meaning, gives teachers a wonderful picture by characterising creating as ordering, and therefore, "giving things meaning" and "calling them to life."[24] Gert Biesta distinguishes seven essential factors of good and risky education: *creating, communication, teaching, learning, emancipation, democracy, and virtuosity.*[25] It is interesting that Biesta finds these aspects of risky education in the *vulnerability* of the open class situation. In this way, Biesta accentuates the valuable quality of a *teaching of openness, of vulnerability* (not to be confused with the term *weak schools* used by the state, in Holland).

Block education that arises out of consciously practiced vulnerability, out of openness therefore, has the potential for fresh interaction spontaneously welling up, and for inspired lessons. Such lessons are experienced by the students as wellsprings for their further life. The vulnerability of education should not be viewed as a problem that needs to be solved by more precisely prescribed methods and instruction, but rather as the transparent dimension that makes valuable pedagogical practice possible, because it helps put the students into the world as new and fresh individuals. Biesta: *"Thus the vulnerability of education demonstrates that all educational practice—both of those who teach and those who are taught—always carries a risk."*[26]

4

Traveling through Land of Blocks

THE PERSPECTIVE OF A TRAVELING TEACHER

In this chapter I will show by means of one of my own block lessons how the content and form of this method of teaching creates opportunities for autonomous, creative activities for both the teacher and the students. In this sense it is intentional "risky education."

When as a teacher you decide to travel through Blockland to meet students there, you embark on the adventure of a lifetime. Block teaching is an essential part of the Waldorf curriculum. What determines the value of this essential part of Waldorf education? The intention of block teaching is to engage the student in his entire being, as a doing, feeling and thinking human being. How do you, as the traveler, meet, address and invite the inhabitants in such a way that you can explore the landscape with them and work in it together for a while? In spite of the magnificence and diversity of the landscape there are experiences gained and itineraries laid out by prior travelers that can be helpful.

For instance, block teaching has a distinct structure to bring this to realization. In every block we have a threefold objective, namely to create a process in which the students move from understanding to experiencing, and on to processing, working with the material. The block begins by recalling the material of the previous day that is then shared, discussed and deepened. Thereafter new material is introduced by the teacher in a living and multi-sided manner, and experienced together with the students. Finally, the students work with the material in an individual way, in writing or artistically.

I will illustrate this process using one of my own journeys on which, together with 11th-graders, I explored Medieval literature in the form of the story of Parsifal. In the following I will give a detailed description of the architecture of the lesson and the ways of working; I will also go into the pedagogical intentions underlying the whole approach.

The Beginning of the Lesson

At the door I greet the students of the 11th grade. It is

a sunny Wednesday morning, we are feeling like getting going. We shake hands, make a few friendly and considerate comments about each other and are cheerful. Together we put the tables and chairs in a square; that feels nicer and more intimate. At the blackboard I have a lot of colored crayons and fat white chalk. After a brief conversation we are ready for the morning verse; we stand and, just like every morning, we say the opening verse together:

I look into the world,
Wherein there shines the sun;
Wherein there gleam the stars.
The plants, they live and grow,
The beasts, they feel and live,
And man to spirit gives
A dwelling in his soul.
I look into the soul
That dwells within me.
God's spirit lives and moves
In light of sun and soul,
In heights of worlds without,
In depths of soul within.
Spirit of God,
To Thee I seeking turn,
That strength and grace and skill
For learning and for work
In me may live and grow.
　　—Rudolf Steiner

The purpose of the beginning of the lesson is to gradually create a feeling of shared attention and involvement with the educational process. The students are received by the teacher at the door of the class, and the teacher shakes the hand of each student. Every day starts with saying the school verse together. The lesson often begins with a warming-up and tuning-in by means of a song, poem or movement exercise.

THE PHASE OF UNDERSTANDING

Recalling the Content of the Previous Day

The students sit down. I walk around a bit and ask one of the students to ask a classmate to read to us what he or she wrote down from the content of the previous day. The selected student is happy to do that and reads from his main lesson book about the father of Parsifal on whom the culture of Baghdad made a deep impression. In the end, Ghamuret, the father, fell in a battle for his friend, the caliph of Baghdad. As they listen to the text of their classmate, the other students compare it with their own work. They thus discover different accents in the freely written texts. If anything is not clear or when there are questions we discuss them and resolve them together.

Individual Understanding out of a Joint Process

Then we speak about Baghdad in the ninth century. It is the time of Al Mamun, the son and successor of the legendary Harun al Rashid, a time when Jews, Hellenistic philosophers and Christians were tolerated and respected in this Islamic city. With its universities, public libraries and hospital, this city, we conclude together, was as the New York of its time. This last remark brings questions and reactions of surprise. The students compare the situation with our time, the Baghdad of today—after the destructive war and years of conservative Islam—with this tolerance and prosperity of twelve hundred years ago. Out of the shared experience of an open conversation a new view of Islam develops. It is a factual experience that arose from the time and space for a conversation and from the relationship to the lesson content of the previous day, together with the experience gained by its artistic processing in the main lesson book.

Deepening Conceptual Understanding by Artistic Processing

We conclude the discussion and move to deepen a particular aspect of the story. As the teacher I always extensively prepare this deepening. Today we are considering the manner in which Ghamuret, the father of Parsifal, was killed. He was involved in a fight outside the gates of Baghdad and was hit by a spear in his forehead. In Wolfram von Eschenbach's version of the Parsifal story such things are quite precisely described. It is the reason why this version is recommended for the eleventh grade in the curriculum of the Waldorf school. The spear hits Ghamuret in his forehead exactly between the eyebrows. In my deepening I want to go into this point, not so much by speaking about it, but by making a drawing. The main lesson book has pages of good quality, both for writing and for drawing. Everyone gives his main lesson book its own form and makes his own choices for composition, use of color or black-and-white, and also as to handwriting, calligraphy and lay-out of the text.

I am drawing on the blackboard and the students make a similar drawing in their own way in their main lesson book. We are drawing a face showing the spot between the eyes where Ghamuret was hit by the spear. What is it about this spot, this place of concentration? We are drawing a shiny or concentrated spot in that place, the third eye. As we are drawing we practice to experience this point. One student makes an association with a concentration exercise for dyslectics according to the Ron Davies method. With many students, and also for me at the blackboard, the drawing becomes more and more expressive. Free artistic work deepens the experience and insight without fixing it; it creates space for one's own personal experience.

The content and written processing of the lesson material of the previous day is recapitulated during a dialogue in the class. By explicitly looking back on concepts and content that were learned earlier, we not only activate knowledge that is already there, but we also make comparisons in time possible and we stimulate a careful build-up of conceptual content.

The purpose of the repetition and discussion of the previous day's content is to take a fresh look, after a night has passed, at what was taken in. In this way the process of "bringing things to life anew in the memory" is applied consciously as a didactic means for deepening and autonomous conceptual understanding. This is also the reason why blocks of several weeks are given daily in the morning. Everything is then still close to the time of awaking, and the processing that happens in the night is still close to the surface. The idea behind creating space for the deepening effect of the night is to offer the students better access to their own insight, judgment and intuition.[27]

JUDGING AUTONOMOUSLY

From this review deepening and clarifying questions will arise. In the resulting discussion the lesson content and its processing can lead to new points of view and experiences, for which the main lesson book, where the lesson content of the previous day was processed, serves as an aid. *"Thinking is a process in which concepts and ideas arise. The concept cannot be obtained from the observation, but is added to the observation. Observation stimulates thinking, and by means of thinking we can connect one observation with another."*[28]

The central purpose of this discussion is for the students

to gain insights and experiences autonomously. The teacher holds back as much as possible, but is eager to hear the input and discoveries of the students. The goal is to let the students arrive at a free and deepening conceptual understanding on their own. The ultimate objective of this first part of the lesson is that they develop autonomous judgments, especially in the higher grades. In the collectivity of the class they get to know each other's discoveries, questions and insights and can deepen them in a sincere and open conversation. After John Dewey, Biesta points to the generative and creative value of radically open and indeterminate communication. He concludes that the prerequisite for such communication lies in participation, in doing things together.

Developing conceptual understanding is treated as a process in block teaching, a hermeneutic process. This is an activity in which gaining knowledge, philosophy and art find each other. It views the human being as one who interprets as he interacts with other human beings, things, events and himself. This is visible in the encounter of the students with the lesson material, in the dialog they have with each other and within themselves, but also from the manner in which each of them individually, but at the same time connected with each other, continue the dialog in their drawings. The authentic will to understand and the ability to see through texts, stories and art is characteristic for the entire existence of humanity in the world.

THE PHASE OF EXPERIENCING

Experiencing Stories

Now it is time for a new part of the story. I have prepared for this in detail, but tell the story freely, from memory. The students listen and make notes. As I am telling the story I use the blackboard to write down important concepts and keywords. The story is about Parsifal's childhood years. He grows up alone with his mother and a few servants on a distant estate. Parsifal is a child of the open air, he is always out in the forest and the fields. His mother always calls him "dear boy." It is the only name he knows.

One day, he makes a bow and aims a self-made arrow on a bird. He hits the bird and it falls down. Parsifal runs toward it, throws it up in the air and exclaims: "Fly again!" But the bird is dead and falls down. Parsifal runs to his mother who tells him the following, entirely in the spirit of the Middle Ages: "God gives life, and God takes life." Parsifal asks: "What is God?" His mother replies:"God is more light than the day!" "Then I want to become like God," is his conclusion, for he feels dark and somber, something he had not known before.

The precise choice of my words, as the teacher telling the story, matters. For example, the question "What is God?" and not "Who is God?" indicates that until then he has not received any concept of God or religion at all from his mother. This will create a great topic of discussion tomorrow. Also the darkness he experiences, and the longing for light, are possible subjects of conversation for students of the ages of 16 and 17. Whether or not this actually happens—I always let that depend on the moment and on the questions of the students. I have a ready list of many themes for discussion in the back of my head.

Today's story culminates in the unexpected encounter with three knights in the forest. Parsifal sees a great, shining light. He jumps out of the bushes and exclaims: "Are you God?" The sun on the armor of the three knights on their horses is blinding. The knights laugh and tell him they are knights of King Arthur. Parsifal's resolution stands firm: he too can become lighter than the day as a knight of King Arthur!

Free Narration: from Story to Imagination

In this phase of the block lesson the emphasis is on freely experiencing lesson contents, and the teacher has the role of the inspirer and storyteller. From the beginning, telling stories has formed an integral part of block teaching.[29] Free rendition is deemed to be the most effective form of bringing new lesson material. The spoken word then gets completely free play, and the teacher himself creates his own lessons and speaks freely about the lesson contents. Any potential methodologies and textbooks remain in the background so they do not come between the teacher and the students. "*First I tell the children some facts, the facts that take place in space and time ... Afterward I characterize.*"[30]

Enthusiasm was for Steiner an important prerequisite for good education. He meant the enthusiasm with which the teacher presents the lesson content to the students, as a result of which the enthusiasm of the students is also aroused.[31] Block teaching is particularly suited for this. Interest is aroused not just by the content of the teaching, but especially also by the person of the teacher and his personal connection with the subject he is bringing.

By means of freely related stories and graphic examples the lesson content is brought alive, in order to convey the lesson content in a living manner without nailing it down intellectually too firmly. Listening attentively to a story awakens love for a particular subject. By concentrated attention on the story as they are listening the students wake up to the understanding and concepts that are still hiding in them. And in attentive listening to a freely told story their own pictures remain mobile and imaginative. The purpose is to create the possibility for authentically and autonomously formed experiences, pictures and insights in the students.

In this phase of the lesson the students are addressed particularly in the way they experience and observe, not so much in their intellectual understanding. The focus is on content and dialog. The student practices to observe and describe the experiences offered him through the phenomenological approach. The idea is that in this way the student intensifies the experiences without jumping right away to conceptual understanding. The pedagogical intention is to awaken presence of mind by creating opportunities for the students' own experiences in a broad spectrum of observations and perceptions through the lesson content. This pedagogy of experience aims to foster "living thinking" in the students. Living thinking fills itself with ensouled and imaginative thoughts.[32]

The importance of telling stories is being increasingly endorsed in educational circles. This is not only because of the value stories may have in making connections between cultures and individuals, but also because of the value for an individual to empathize and to mirror himself in the experiences of another person.[33] One study of the importance of telling stories in education concluded that, when students hear and live into stories they are told, they come into a creative learning process that leads to their acquiring their own insights. Michael Schiro identifies the added value of telling stories as part of giving explanations in teaching mathematics:

> It is within my experience one of the most important qualities of the effects of stories, provided they are freely told, that they give a person the possibility to process contents autonomously and authentically by inner activity in an entirely personal manner.[34]

Other studies have focused on storytelling as an instrument to stimulate moral development. I attach particular value for my work in the class to the idea that the story not only conveys knowledge, but also makes a moral experience possible:

28

I assume that one of the primary functions of narrative in culture is to endow a certain sequence of events with moral meaning.[35]

THE PROCESSING PHASE

Autonomous Processing of the New Lesson Material

The students now get some time to work on the text in their own words in their main lesson books. This allows them to re-experience the story as it was told, and to reflect on what they heard and experienced in their own way. After some time I let them arrange the tables in groups and give them a picture of Sir Galahad, a knight of King Arthur, in shining armor. They can use the picture as inspiration to develop their own artistic processing of the story by making drawings, paintings, collages or in any other way they choose. A nice, cozy atmosphere of creativity then grows until the end of the lesson.

It is the intention of Waldorf education to achieve a pedagogy of closeness, in which the initial distance between the individual and the phenomena in the world is bridged by artistically processing one's experience of those phenomena. In the course of such processing the students connect with the phenomenon out of their feeling life. These experiences and capacities are expected to contribute to the willingness and ability to accept trust and love as ethical foundations of social life.[36]

In the last part of the lesson the students work independently on processing the lesson content and practicing their skills. This written and artistic, creative work with the lesson content offers the pedagogical opportunity to process the lesson content in their own authentic manner using their own pictures and images. Steiner taught that in the world of morality intuition follows directly on observation. When you acquire the capacity to create images, you also develop the ability to take in moral intuitions.[37]

The Main Lesson Book and Creative Writing

This independent work through pictures mostly takes place in the main lesson book which is used as a workbook and journal. The main lesson book was developed especially for the Waldorf schools and is used worldwide in these schools. It has both lined and blank pages for writing and drawing. The book, which grows into a personal workbook, gives the student a place to think through and live into the lesson content and thus make it his own in an authentic, personal way. Both written texts and artistic, picture-based methods are used to give expression to the conceptual understanding the student gradually develops.

In the main lesson book the student works with the lesson material by factual descriptions in words and pictures as he has perceived it, thus out of the way he experienced it himself and out of the meanings he sees in it. For the written texts you might think of a summary of the story told by the teacher, or a report of the steps involved in an experiment the student made himself, accompanied by drawings. The artistic processing forms might consist of a descriptive reflection of the story, or the story might be worked into a poem, a drawing to show the essence of the lesson, or a self-designed research project.

During the block lesson the students do a lot of writing. Beginning with the higher grades in the lower school, the students get the freedom to elaborate in their main lesson books on the lesson contents given by the teacher, in their own words and in their own ways. In this way they exercise in the course of the years not only the technique of writing, but also the creative process of working with the material in a thinking manner.

Creative writing is first of all first creative thinking. Being able to write means being articulate, able to reflect one's own ideas and thoughts, values and convictions to others.

By writing creatively you discover your own voice; this is extraordinarily important for one's own inner personal development.[38]

The results of this daily creative writing in the book are formative for the total personality.

If necessary, the student finishes the daily processing of the lesson material after school. At the end of the block this book has become an individual piece of work and reference book of the student. At the end of the block the student (often) puts an evaluation of the content and quality of the block in the book, as well as a self-evaluation focused on insight, processing, attitude and appreciation. The book and the (self)evaluation are reviewed by the teacher, who adds constructive comments concerning the knowledge gained, attitude and developmental process of the student. These comments form the basis for the report card later. Most students keep their main lesson books and consider them later as precious possessions.

Conclusion and Transition to the Following Block Lesson

I conclude the lesson with the assignment to finish the work on the lesson before tomorrow (to the extent needed), and to think about the question of why Parsifal grew up so alone with his mother, and what examples of this they are familiar with from their own surroundings or in society at large.

After the classroom has been put back in order, tables and chairs returned to their places and wiped, and the blackboard has been erased, we say goodbye and shake hands again at the door. I ask some students something personal or about the other lessons that day, or any other current things. Because our school has about 650 students, it is still just possible for the students and teachers to meet personally and know each other.

31

5

Experiencing Blocks in "Blockland"

"The block lessons are very informative; I remember what I learn much more easily, because you hear it first, then make notes, and afterward work on it further. It is also nice to make a main lesson book; you work to make it really pretty. It is very creative and it is great to stay with a subject for a longer time so that you can really immerse yourself in it. It is also a nice, quiet beginning of the day."

"History Block: Long live the revolution!"

I now invite you to let the inhabitants of this land be your guides, just as I did myself. Walk with them through Blockland and let them show you the viewpoints they have discovered during their many years there and find important enough to share with you.

VIEWPOINT I: VALUABLE LEARNING EXPERIENCES

Current students are outspoken in their appreciation of block teaching. More than in most other lessons, interest in the lesson material is aroused during the block lessons. They especially appreciate the "special" blocks, such as drama, but also subject blocks such as astronomy, projective geometry, Parsifal, or poetry, which have contents that are not present in the daily subject lessons. Sometimes, however, the highest grades experience a block as less relevant. They may also view blocks that fall outside the state mandated tests (in schools following government mandates) as a chance for a broad developmental education.

"You keep getting subjects that are not included in the tests; those make it easier to recognize connections between things and you create more general knowledge."

"I think it is very good to learn things about subjects that are not part of the tests."

"In the blocks you learn more general things that are dealt with in more detail in the subject lessons."

"You receive a lot that has nothing to do with the tests—more often than not what at first looked like the 'most useless' blocks are the most fun."

The students experience that the sustained attention, which becomes possible because you are focused on a certain subject during two successive lesson periods for several weeks, makes a very close connection with the subject possible, and deepens the experience of the subject.

"I really like the fact that in the blocks you can, as it were, immerse yourself in the subject. It gives you more time and opportunity to understand it."

"In the blocks I am always aware that we get into the material in more depth. I then put more time and effort into it and am better focused, because we have an hour and a half instead of just three quarters of an hour."

Whether a block is experienced by the students as "fun," "good," or "meaningful" depends to a large extent on the way the teacher approaches this way of teaching. Lessons in which the teachers display enthusiasm and in which they do many things themselves—such as experiments and artistic work—are appreciated; this is not the case for blocks in which the emphasis is on the transfer of knowledge by the teacher.

"... differs block by block; I think chemistry, biology, drama, for example, are a good balance."

"When the teacher talks for an hour and a half I find the block very long, but when we can do things too, then I like it; then the block seems really short."

"I really like the blocks very much, but the subject lessons are also important. I find subject lessons that are given like blocks tedious, because subject lessons have to be clear and explicit, with books. Sometimes I learn more from the block, sometimes more from the subject lessons. It depends on the way they are given."

Block Lesson Education

Research has been done in the English speaking world into the value of block lesson education.[39] In the United States block education is given at high school level in blocks of 90 minutes. In some schools the whole day is divided into such blocks instead of the usual lesson periods of 45 to 50 minutes.

This is different in Waldorf schools where both forms are used side by side. In this context block education is more a didactic form, and not so much a form for pedagogical content. The value of this didactic form seems to be that it creates an openness for more contact between students and teacher, more time for scientific experiments, and more space for the teacher. There seem to be less stress, fewer failing grades and fewer dropouts.

There are also critics of block education. One criticism is that there are too few moments in the week for exercises. Some subjects, such as mathematics and languages, need daily exercises. Another criticism is that much of the lesson material from a previous block is forgotten, as also happens during summer vacation. Another problem is that not all students are able to remain focused throughout the longer time span of a block lesson. The comments by the students in our school demonstrate that they not only share the positive experiences with the students who are taught in block lessons, but also a number of the criticisms.

"A disadvantage can be that you have the same subject for a lot of hours. Or the subject in the subject lesson differs from that in the block, which may be confusing, especially in the case of math."

"I think the block is really part of the Waldorf school. In a block we do more creative things. But sometimes I find that I do not remember all the material of the block. I don't know what the reason is."

Viewpoint II: Time for the Self

In 1903 Henri Bergson wrote his book *The Creative Mind: An Introduction into Metaphysics*. Rudolf Steiner, his contemporary, appreciated his thinking.[40] Bergson did research into our experience of time out of two aspects of the I. He made a distinction between the *daily I* and the *profound I*, the deeper I, the true self. The daily self experiences itself as bound to clock time, whereas the true self experiences time as free space. The experience of freedom offers space for intuition within the personal experience and the knowledge process. Experience out of the true self creates a more spacious concept of time; Bergson called it *pure duration*. It appears that it is this experience of rest, this different experience of time, that is created by block education. In the descriptions of their experiences of block teaching, students notably often mention quiet in conjunction with deepening into a particular subject.

"In the morning there is quiet. For me this quiet is very important—catch your breath. It also makes the contact and bond with the teacher better."

"I find the block a nice and quiet beginning of the day."

"I like the block lessons; it is a little more quiet and you have more time."

"I always think that the time flies! I also really like the way the lesson is organized; there is time and no need to hurry so with everything."

Students connect the experience of quiet and deepening with their personal connection and absorption of the lesson contents.

"You go into a particular subject more deeply and therefore dedicate more attention and time to it, with the result that you retain it better."

"Block teaching creates a kind of quiet and order in the day, a distinct beginning. It is nice to be completely immersed in a particular subject for a longer period of time. It becomes easier to see connections."

What stands out is that this "retaining" does not so much refer to factual knowledge of the subject, but rather comprehension and insight into the ways in which the content that was experienced relates to other themes, experiences and insights. In this sense block education contributes to a broad development of the students. It enables them to absorb and connect with a diverse palette of lesson contents and, in the process, also has a formative influence on the personalities of the students. Viewed in this way, block education is an example of what Socrates called "the art of the midwife;" as a person brings his own conceptual understanding into the world, his personality unfolds at the same time.

"I think that the broad range of all the different blocks makes a big contribution to my personal development."

"For me block education is more personal. We can discover many things ourselves, which also enables us to give them our own 'twist.'"

"... the freedom of being able to use my own creativity and ideas."

"I think that block education is good for your personal development ... the same class ... familiar environment ... feeling at home ... being more yourself ... drawing ... making your own main lesson book ... you learn through different parts of your brain."

"... by immersing yourself in stories and possibly finding ways to apply them in your own life."

VIEWPOINT III: SPACE FOR GENUINE ENCOUNTERS WITH EACH OTHER

Emmanuel Levinas spoke of the encounter with the irreplaceable individual in each human being as *the face of the other*, in which the uniqueness of the individuality expresses itself.[41] When at the beginning of the lesson, especially at the beginning of the day upon entry and at the beginning of the block, student and teacher shake hands, this is experienced as a potential moment for an encounter of equals. The new arrival and the experienced traveler meet with respect.

"What I like is that you really create a kind of personal connection with the teachers, which also means that you get more out of the lessons."

In the hand, and also in the look into each other's eyes, that which lives in the face of the other makes a brief appearance. This personal gesture creates the possibility for the deeper self, irrespective of differences in social standing or age, to manifest itself in a brief, timeless moment.

"Shaking the teacher's hand before the lesson. This makes you more an equal with the person who teaches you. I think that because of this I have begun to treat more people as my equals, not only as regards age, but also socially."

Block education in high school generally takes place in socially heterogeneous groups. Students with a variety of talents and levels of intelligence are daily together in the block at the beginning of the day. The students in our school consider this a positive and valuable aspect.

"We have students from all kinds of different programs in our class. With this class you go through the blocks throughout the 12 grades. You therefore learn to get along with others who are not at your own level."

"... that you keep having all subjects with your own class for 12 years. Super important. The learning process is very much a joint exercise."

The lessons offer the possibility of having discussions with each other and with the teacher. According to the students this helps them to develop different perspectives on things, and to become familiar with different qualities and levels of learning. During these hours they do not so much experience how they differ from each other, how quickly or effectively they are able to learn new lesson materials or skills, but the natural and very individual ways in which each of them experiences, processes, represents in pictures or words what they meet in the lessons.

"Because all of us, all at different levels, are together in the block, I think that I have been able to develop my social skills better. For I think that different people of different levels also have different qualities and problems. "

Despite the differences in programs followed by the students, many of them remain friends throughout their school years, and even thereafter. This is an important aspect of learning in a cohesive group. This creates a strong, intensely human connection among the students. Block teaching, therefore, has an unmistakable social value; students can show themselves in all their differences, they learn to rub shoulders with each other every day and to understand each other's ways of learning and views of life.

VIEWPOINT IV: DEEP, PERSONAL CONCEPTUAL UNDERSTANDING

The students describe block teaching in the Waldorf high school as a didactic form of working that leads to a deeper comprehension of the lesson material. They indicate that they experience in the blocks, more than in the other lessons, the potential to arrive at their own conceptual understanding, and that this understanding goes beyond that in the other lessons, and is also more lasting.

"In the blocks I understand the subject very well, and it stays longer with me."

Block education is experienced as a haven of quiet amid the busy stream of daily education. Philosopher Matthew

Crawford states that humanity is in an attention crisis.[42] Because of the fragmentation of life it is difficult for young people to keep focused on something for a longer period of time. Crawford pleads for doing and experiencing things on our own, based on research into *embodied cognition* which shows that we do not get to know the world just by observing it as an outsider, but especially by actively doing things in it. He asks us to strengthen our connection with the reality around us and to bring about a feeling of belonging together.

The students make a connection between their development of conceptual understanding and several different characteristics of block education. The specific practices used, including the free presentation of the lesson material by the teacher, contribute to their conceptual understanding.

"Especially the stories, questions or assignments that lead you deeper into the material also very often stimulate the brain."

"Knowledge was addressed during storytelling and working on the text, while experience and activity were emphasized during drawing and other creative activities."

Another helpful aspect that the students frequently mentioned is that block teaching focuses their attention for a longer time on one particular subject. In this way they experience that they have great potential to arrive at their own conceptual understanding.

"Block education gives me more time and opportunity to understand the lesson material."

"I like block teaching because you are busy with one subject for a certain length of time. This makes it easier to understand and absorb the material better."

For the students this better understanding is connected with the fact that the blocks are focused on a specific aspect of a subject.

"... that in the block you go more deeply into a specific aspect of the subject and stay with it for some time."

The students connect such conceptual understanding through deepening with a qualitative change in their own judgment capacity. They experience that block teaching brings more perspective in their judgment capacity.

"Because you learn to immerse yourself deeply into something you can look at things in real life from different angles, before you judge too quickly."

J. Schieren depicts conceptual understanding in block education as a productive activity by which the integration of subject and object, of self and world, is realized in an increasing context of meaning.[43]

VIEWPOINT V: THE IMPORTANCE OF FREE PROCESSING TIME

The students also see a connection between deeper comprehension and the invitation implied in the ways of working during the block lessons to develop their own kinds of experience and processing. The process of being able to work creatively on your own is experienced as contributing to arriving at conceptual understanding. Blocks are experienced by students as a developmental process in which their own creativity has free play.

"The learning process ... I can ask anything if I need to, and otherwise I get to work myself."

"You can be really creative in it. I really experience the block as a growth process; every day you make a step in the direction of comprehension."

"The block has more depth and room for expressing creativity."

"... freedom to express creativity and ideas."

The work in and on the main lesson book is an important

part of this. The fact that learning does not come out of an existing textbook, but that you make your own textbook in the form of the main lesson book of the block is something most students like.

"There was always a lot of freedom in your own way of processing; the lesson material itself was fixed."

"Processing in the main lesson book is autonomous in the sense that you can put your own ideas into it. At least, that's how it is for me. You have to process the lesson material yourself, and that gives you a sense of independence. You have to make your own choices as to how you are going to do it."

"For me the main lesson book is a very good means to really absorb the lesson material. It gives me room to express my own picture and imagination, and I happen to like drawing very much. For this reason I like to do my best on the whole thing."

"In the block you also practice writing texts and giving your creativity free play in them."

Rudolf Steiner worked on the premise of the unique identity of each human being,[44] the origin of which lies in every person's capacity to carry a free individuality.[45] He therefore viewed the students' individual processing of the lesson material as an important aspect of block teaching.[46] The main lesson book makes autonomous and authentic processing of the lesson material possible. This processing, which has to be vigorous, independent and creative, makes a deep impression and demonstrates personal development. This is also experienced by the students and they recognize it in the way they have themselves processed the lesson material in their books.

"I really like making the main lesson book beautiful, and I see it a little bit as a piece of myself."

"A main lesson book has great value for me, I keep them all! It is fun to look back and see how you have grown in all respects."

"I really like leafing through my main lesson books and see how I have developed."

One of the objectives of Waldorf education is to create opportunities for the students to express their own creativity and discover the meaning of things in their own way. Longhand writing in the main lesson book is a form of independent processing of the lesson material and developing their own insights. Among other things, their writing in the book generates attention.[47]

The objective of the writing process in the main lesson book, certainly for older students, is to be a creative one, a process in which they express in words what they have experienced, their pictures, and recognition of meaning. In this sense a creative writing process encompasses more than "creative writing" which is rather about writing stories, diaries or poems. *"Creative writing for young people in high school? Wait a minute—that is not part of the regular classes, is it? Is it mandatory? But it is not part of the State requirements!" "No, but it is so relaxing, so inspiring, so good for the self-confidence of the students."*[48]

All these methods of creative writing can also be found in the main lesson book as ways of processing the content of the block. Research among Dutch high school students shows that they are fond of writing creatively, for instance, in the form of their own stories or poems.[49] This is also true for our own students; when the book is used to let them write freely they indicate that they derive great satisfaction from that.

VIEWPOINT VI: WORKING WITH THE AVAILABLE TIME

Students have less satisfaction in the block lessons when they feel that they do not have enough free time. When that happens they experience an implicit, or explicit, demand to absorb the lesson material as given. They experience this as limiting their own ability to process it freely. This seems especially to be the case when the lesson material is treated as preparation for a test. Reporting literally what the teacher told them is for them less interesting and relevant than processing in which they express their own experiences, perspective and insights. But they do indicate that when the material is "exciting" they feel more motivated as they are processing it in the main lesson book.

Together with the opportunity to process the lesson content on their own, the students also feel a responsibility to make good use of it. They sense expectations both from themselves and from the teachers that they have to meet. Sometimes those expectations work as motivators, sometimes they have to wrestle with them. However, the choice of how they will act is always theirs to make.

"When I like the block, and the teacher appreciates it when you make an effort to be creative, then I do that and also like to do it; the main lesson book then has great value for me."

"It is annoying when I can't get it to be pretty, and I think some teachers set their demands too high and don't give enough freedom in the way you form it."

"In my opinion, making the main lesson book often takes too much time. It demands a lot of attention."

"I am not very creative in the way I go about my main lesson book. I mostly stick to the examples on the blackboard."

Having to work on a self-developed textbook can also be an obstacle, for example, when you have missed something due to illness, or when things in the block have not become clear. Students also indicate that sometimes they need more clarity as to the expectations and objectives of a block in order to give the main lesson book a good form. Lesson processing in this book does take a lot of time, and therefore they find it important that it can take place as much as possible within the timeframe of the block.

VIEWPOINT VII: THE IMPORTANCE OF INTUITION

In order to discover how students view conceptual understanding I have had a focused discussion with ten of our 17-year-old students. The following statement about conceptual understanding is characteristic for their collective idea:

"Conceptual understanding does not come in as words or formulas; it is more a kind of haze of information. It is less easy to reproduce or explain because it can't be reduced to words; it is rather a kind of feeling that leads to understanding."

From the descriptions of the students emerges a picture of conceptual understanding as a strongly intuitive process. Sadler Smith describes intuition as a process of knowing in which one at once sees through the thing.[50] Intuitive learning is a form of learning in which the autonomy of the learning person is fundamental.

"The intuitive learning process is characterized by quick thinking processes during which you try out various thinking approaches and strategies."[51]

It is my experience that intuition is eminently personal. Confidence in yourself and in the process seems to be one of the prerequisites to awaken intuitive capacities. Young people can find this confidence when they meet teachers who give them confidence, and who meet the world with confidence. A cooperating factor is that the teacher—unknown to the student—does not work toward a specific outcome, but in the whole process of observing and characterizing remains open to new insights, which may turn up with the students as intuitions. When young people then have the opportunity to admit these intuitions of their own and trust them, they receive a gift for life, which has everything to do with self-confidence and autonomy.

VIEWPOINT VIII: FORMING CONCEPTUAL UNDERSTANDING—A VULNERABLE PROCESS

Because developing conceptual understanding is such an eminently intuitive and personal process, it is also experienced as a delicate and vulnerable one. The way the students experience it, it runs the risk of being unable to attain enough depth if the student does not get sufficient opportunity for personal expression, for instance, because of time pressure or the necessity to prepare for a test. Then the outcome of block education narrows to a transfer of knowledge of pre-existing concepts, which the students feel is unsatisfying.

"There is a certain amount of material we have to master within a certain amount of time. This means that there is no space for discovering and learning on our own, but we have to develop understanding the same way we do it in the subject lessons for a test. I have the idea that there is a big gap between thinking broadly and thinking narrowly in the Waldorf school. Waldorf pedagogy especially wants to stimulate broad thinking, but the test demands much narrow thinking." (an 11th grade student)

"The acquisition of knowledge may dominate to such an extent that you lose sight of your direction, or you have too much to absorb, so that perception does not come about at the same pace ... that deep comprehension has to exist!" (an 11th grade student)

Deep, personal comprehension is hard to arrive at when the many impressions received in the lesson (in a story, observation of an experiment, experience or from a text) cannot be processed at a quiet pace. Following Steiner, Schieren points to the processing of observations and experiences in an easy atmosphere as a prerequisite for a gradual process toward forming judgments and thus ultimately toward reaching a living comprehension.[52] Sommer emphasizes the importance of a phenomenological approach to the world and the personality as a necessary didactic means for block education in order to be able to arrive at qualitative conceptual understanding.[53] He states that this phenomenological approach makes dynamic changes in perspective possible, and thus also a broader and more personal conceptual understanding.

6

Looking Back on My Journey with the Guides along the Viewpoints

When I look back on what I have learned on my tour along the viewpoints, for which the students were my guides, the following picture emerges of their life in Blockland.

The statements of our guides reflect great enthusiasm for block education, for the stories, the artistic processing of the lesson material and experiences, the chance to freely develop

49

your own insights and give expression to them in your own words, pictures and ways of working. Plato already connected enthusiasm with inspiration.* This enthusiasm seems to be especially related to the openness felt by the students to engage in their own creative processes.

In the eyes of the current inhabitants of Blockland the experiences they gain in this land have an exceptional quality of quiet and creative space. In our future meetings in Blockland it is important always to keep in mind the general, formative aspect and the students' own free, creative space, since these create the opportunity to meet the students' need to develop deeper conceptual understanding which, in turn, enables them to recognize relationships between greater themes in the world. The fact that they become familiar with a wide diversity of subjects, skills and insights in the lesson materials, but also in the traveling teachers and fellow inhabitants, contributes to this. Of course, this also holds true for the different ways of working; the alternating appeals to thinking, feeling and will are helpful in this regard because the students can thus meet and experience themselves and the world in different ways.

The encounter with the other, be it a person or an idea, is a valuable aspect of a stay in Blockland. Out of a foundation of attention for stories, out of enthusiasm, and out of creative processes, inspiration and creative receptivity for intuition light up in an autonomous process of gaining knowledge. This creates the potential of developing profound conceptual understanding. The main lesson book is an important instrument in this process, both to help the students to experience and process the lesson material so they can create something new out of it, and also to look back later and see how they have developed.

---

* The word *enthusiasm* comes from the Greek and indicates the god (*theos*) within (*en*).

When we really intensively contemplate the landscapes the students share with us on the viewpoints, we are able to observe a number of pointers for us, the traveling teachers.

- The broad range of subjects makes Blockland interesting and inviting to live in. Don't ignore it!

- In the morning the inhabitants want to experience the space to look around open-mindedly and work with scientific experiments, listen to stories, and process their experiences in their own ways and with great independence. In the subject lessons later in the day more specific knowledge and skills can be learned and practiced.

- The inhabitants are quality conscious and expect of the traveling teachers that they inspire them; this usually indeed happens, but it does always demand attention.

- Continue to give block teaching broadly through the classes across different levels of intelligence and talents.

- Especially by being allowed to let go and forget the lesson material, and then coming back to it the next day, the experience is enriched and the understanding becomes deeper and more personal. For this reason, processing needs to happen as much as possible during the morning hours.

Viewed from the perspective of the students, the experiences they gain in Blockland seem akin to what in educational circles is sometimes called "slow education."

"Slow education—doing everything as well as possible instead of as fast as possible."[54]

"Slow education is also about connection to knowledge and to learning, real learning. Slow education is about supporting our children to develop values and ethics that will enable

them to live a joyous life in the slow lane." [55]

*"Mostly the block is just fun. You have time to really get into
the subjects, and there are no books at all. The greatest thing is
when the teachers tell beautiful stories in the block, but that is
of course just Waldorf!"*

*"Because you learn to delve into something you can look at
everything in real life from different angles, before you jump
into a judgment too quickly."*

*"It is great to be completely immersed in a subject for a longer
period of time; it helps you to see connections between things."*

*"The way I see things in the world has changed enormously,
and I have developed a positive mind set."*

In a recent educational journal slow education was
described as a valuable teaching method:

*"The future of young people in today's complex society makes
it important to challenge and teach them in creative and
personal ways. What counts in the process is not just the
outcome but especially the path of learning in the direction of
this, often overestimated, outcome."* [56]

7

Conclusion: A Story Born from My Travels

My young guides took us on a journey to eight viewpoints in Blockland. Each viewpoint offered a different view on this wide, unique and mysterious land. Mysterious, because the form is simple, whereas the content is so unique and unpredictably broad, because the greatest possible freedom

reigns in this land. The guides give evidence of this freedom during the trip. Their words testify to enthusiasm, but also to profound knowledge of the variation and hidden riches in the landscape.

When as a teacher in a Waldorf school we undertake a journey through Blockland it may happen that the guides ask us to observe the deeper, significant layers in the landscapes they show us. In order to get to know the hidden story behind their statements, we must as travelers be familiar with the geography of Blockland. Just as in other countries, the geography of Blockland can be described in terms of rock formations, rivers and cities.

Blockland has twelve cities in each of which the inhabitants always find their dwelling places for a year. With these cities as their base, the inhabitants make excursions into the surrounding landscape to explore it, work on it and get to know it. The geology of the soil of Blockland may be compared with limestone and granite. The soil has an influence on the way the inhabitants live, what they encounter in the landscape and have to do there, and how they act in their daily existence. There are regions with a lot of limestone where ancient crops and stories can take root in the unpredictable soil, and can be brought to new life by the inhabitants.

There are also areas that consist principally of granite. On the inflexible forms of hard granite the inhabitants have to make experiments to determine what they can build there and how they should do that.

A great river flows through all of Blockland with many side branches. The main river is a mighty stream that connects the very different regions, and the cities within them, with each other, and provides all the cities and regions with the vital fluid that forms the basis of the drive and industry of the students who live in the land and the teachers who travel there. This vital fluid is formed from the living vision of the development of the inhabitants, which wells up from an ancient spring. In the course of twelve years, teachers travel via the main river to all the cities and regions in order to be of service to the inhabitants at the right times.

Although the inhabitants will not often be conscious of the existence of this spring, it is important that in their youthful open-mindedness they continue to be able to feast upon the clear vital fluid that bubbles up from it. Famous schools in antiquity and the Middle Ages were usually situated near a spring. Examples of this are the platonic academy of Chartres, the Carolingian Court School in Aachen (Germany) and Aristotle's school in Miëza (Greece). Each one of these was sought by young people from the entire then known world.

All travelers are required to return regularly to this spring during their journey, not only to experience physically the life-nourishing energy of the spring, but also to care for the spring. In spite of the energy of what it puts into motion, into flow, a spring is also 'weak' and vulnerable, for example, due to pollution, silting up or drying out. Springs therefore need to be cleared from time to time out of the ever-advancing time spirit, with the aid of knowledge and instruments the traveler carries with him. Clearing, opening and testing a spring asks for strength and a willingness to take risks, in order thus to do what is needed and keep the water fresh and flowing. In this way its vital forces are preserved for the inhabitants, the landscape and the travelers.

Endnotes

1. P. Ponte, *Onder zoek met en door leraren* ("Research on and by Teachers"), Book Lemma, 2012.

2. Grounded theory is a systematic methodology in the social sciences involving the construction of theory through methodic gathering and analysis of data. A study using grounded theory is likely to begin with a question, or even just with the collection of qualitative data. As researchers review the data collected, repeated ideas, concepts or elements become apparent, and are tagged with codes, which have been extracted from the data. As more data are collected, and re-reviewed, codes can be grouped into concepts, and then into categories. These categories may become the basis for new theory. Thus, grounded theory is quite different from the traditional model of research, where the researcher chooses an existing theoretical framework, and only then collects data to show how the theory does or does not apply to the phenomenon under study. (Source: wikipedia.org)

3. Rudolf Steiner, *The Spiritual Ground of Education*, GA 305, Anthroposophic Press, 2004.

4. H. Steenbergen, *Vrije en reguliere scholen vergeleken* ("Waldorf and Regular Schools Compared"), State University Groningen, Netherlands, 2009, p. 21.

5. T. Richter, *Pädagigischer Auftrag und Unterrichtsziele—vom Lehrplan der Waldorfschule* ("Educational Mandate and Teaching Objectives—from the Curriculum of the Waldorf School"), Stuttgart, 2016.

6. A. Krijger, *Brede vorming als ruimtescheppend gebeuren* ("Broad Education as Creative Practice"), University of Leiden, 2018.

7. Rudolf Steiner, *Foundations of Human Experience*, GA 293, Anthroposophic Press, 1996.

8. M. Rawson & R. Avinson (ed.), *Towards Creative Teaching: Notes to an Evolving Curriculum for Waldorf Class Teachers*, Floris Books, 2013.

9. Op. cit. note 4.

10. Op. cit. note 8.

11. Op. cit. note 4.

12. G. Biesta, *The Beautiful Risk of Education*, Routledge, 2015.

13. Op. cit. note 7.

14. G. Biesta, *Goed onderwijs, functioneel of disfunctioneel* ("Good Education, Functional or Dysfunctional"), onderwijsmens.nl, 2018.

15. A. Mayo, *Autonomie in verbondenheid* ("Autonomy in Alliance and Connection with Others"), University Leiden, 2015.

16. Op. cit. note 14.

17. Op. cit. note 12.

18. Op. cit. note 7.

19. Rudolf Steiner, *The Philosophy of Freedom*, GA 4, Anthroposophic Press, 1964.

20. G. Lessing, *The Education of the Human Race*, BiblioLife, LLC., n.d.

21. G. Widenmann, *Gedanken über die Unsterblichkeit als Wiederholung des Erdenlebens*, Rarebooksclub.com, 2013.

22. Plato, *The Republic*, trans. B. Jowett, Dover Thrift Editions, 2000.

23. J. Barnes, *The Pre-Socratic Philosophers,* Routledge 1996.

24. J. Caputo, *The Weakness of God*, Indianapolis Press 2006.

25. Op. cit. note 12.

26. Op. cit. note 12.

27. A. Whiel & M. Zech, *Jugendpädagogik in der Waldorfschule*, Kassel, 2017, p. 60.

28. E. Koster, *Fenomenologie als ontvankelijke methode voor de ontmoeting tussen het Ik en de Ander* ("Phenomenology as Receptive Method for the Encounter between the I and the Other"), Radboud University, 2007.

29. Op. cit. note 7.

30. Rudolf Steiner, *Practical Advice to Teachers*, GA 294, Anthroposophic Press, 2000.

31. C. Wiechert, *Het raadsel doorgronden* ("Fathoming the Riddle"), Chicorei, 2017.

32. Op. cit. note 27.

33. J. Bruner, *Making Stories*, Harvard University Press, 2003.

34. M. Schiro, *Curriculum Theory: Conflicting Visions and Enduring Concerns*, Sage Publications, 2007.

35. M. Tappan & M. Packer, *Narrative and Storytelling: Implications for Understanding Moral Development*, Jossey-Bass, 1991.

36. Op. cit. note 27.

37. Op. cit. note 19.

38. S. de Rooij, *Schrijft het voort, creatief schrijven met jongeren* ("Write on! Creative Writing with Young People"), Kunstfactor, 2009.

39. K. Soniat, *Effects of the 4 x 4 Block Schedule on Teacher Behavior and Student Engagement Rate at High School Level*, Louisiana State University, 1999.

40. R. Steiner, *The Riddles of Philosophy*, GA 18, Anthroposophic Press, 1973.

41. E. Levinas, *Totality and Infinity: An Essay on Exteriority*, Pittsburgh Duquesne University Press, 1969.

42. M. Crawford, *The World beyond Your Head,* Farrar, Straus and Giroux, 2015.

43. J. Schieren, "Conclusion, Judgment, Concept: The Quality of Understanding," *Research on Steiner Education* Vol. 1, No. 2.

44. Op. cit. note 7.

45. Op. cit. note 19.

46. Op cit. note 30.

47. M. Kiefer & N. Trummp, "Embodiment Theory and Education: The Foundations of Cognition in Perception and Action,"

Trends in Neuroscience in Education 1(1), 2012.

48. Op. cit. note 38.

49. Op. cit. note 38.

50. S. Smith, *Inside Intuition*, Routledge, 2012.

51. G. Claxton, *Wise up, Learning to Live the Learning Life*, Network Educational Press, 2001.

52. Op. cit. note 43.

53. W. Sommer, "Upper School Teaching at Steiner Waldorf Schools: Cognitive Challenges for the Embodied Self," *Research on Steiner Education* Vol. 1 No. 1.

54. Montrose42blog, montrose42.wordpress.com.

55. "Footprint Choices, Slow Schools and Slow Education—Connecting Children to Life," www.slowmovement.com/slowschools.php.

56. P. Cuijpers, *Het kind, platform voor onderwijs en opvoeding Nivoz*, ("Slow Education and Personalized Learning"), hetkind.org.

Made in the USA
Monee, IL
04 August 2020